ENDITEM.

ENDITEM.

poems

JEREMY ALLAN HAWKINS

Downingfield Press

First published January 2023
Acquired and published January 2024 by
DOWNINGFIELD PRESS PROPRIETARY LIMITED
Suite 346
585 Little Collins Street
Melbourne Victoria 3000

mail@downingfield.com · www.downingfield.com

Downingfield Press undertakes its work on the unceded lands of the Wurundjeri people of the Kulin Nation and pays respect to Elders past, present, and emerging.

ISBN 978-0-6452318-7-8 (paperback)

Cover and book design by M. G. Mader.

NATIONAL LIBRARY OF AUSTRALIA

A catalogue record for this work is available from the National Library of Australia

NOTES AND ACKNOWLEDGEMENTS

This book represents an attempt to transform a corpus of material I originally wrote between 2014 and 2017 as a journalist covering European politics in crisis, a corpus that over time has come to represent, in my eyes, complicity with institutional cruelty. After that period, it became clear to me that I needed to submit that writing to a process of détournment, so as to, on the one hand, break through a false veneer of objectivity, and on the other, to reactivate the text in ways that would reveal already embedded logics at work within. To that end, I started experimenting with a variety of strategies, including text randomizers, collage techniques, erroneous translation, and language filters, varying these predominantly material practices through the different pieces that have now been assembled in this volume. The result is, I think, a text that makes apparent the constant violence of our political discourse, which is in turn transmitted, amplified, and even enacted by the organs and agents of the apparatuses of power. In that sense, this work represents both a kind of testimony and a form of confession. I wish it had less pertinence today than the period in which the source texts were first written, but the sea around which we talked then continues to open and receive.

Many people have made this work possible, with or without meaning to do so, and often in ways that cannot be explained. I offer deep gratitude to Mitchell Mader and Downingfield Press for taking in this work. Also give my heartfelt thanks and solidarity to: Claudine, Alexandre et Etienne, Avni, Mia, David, Nik, Justin, Brett, Whitney, Benjamin, Carrie, Robert, Colin, Johnny, Peter and Heather, Olivier, Vincent, Abigail, Poets & Critics Paris, Jennifer, Lisa, Dimitra, Anna, Tom and Becca, Emma, Janet, John, Frédéric et Tim, Oisín, Alex and Andreea.

Jeremy Allan Hawkins

GLOBAL ECONOMIC FORECAST OPTIMISTIC DESPITE UNCERTAINTY

130 people dead, & in July,
which she confirmed. the much loved

a bad future for the next.
what can companies do? its wish to define itself today

as well as in screenings of Poltergeist,
because from construction, lighting, & favour

of a non-binding motion, the crowd lifted
signs, consulates, the common

good, he explained, optimistic
about the long & repeated.

despite that volatility, uncertainties are not
for future growth, I believe.

another critical is an assassination
slamming its doors—

the spokesperson held particular interests
for debate: "let's not fool

living in poverty & dying
for law enforcement purposes."

reminded of their reforms put forward
in the context of the battle to build
his most regular activity, walls,
a long address to the pharmaceutical companies

showed how the oil price & other talents
have 15 months to transpose men

originating from Sudan.
he observed that many people
since the end of the cold war work
with the archbishop

but also through the original report on mass
violence & persecution, worried parliamentarians.

uncertainties which persist
with other aircraft & in order to put an end to that

we look at robot
incident disappointment, he began

somewhere, enditem. borders,
terrorist threats, procedures to observe

when the University of Paris migrants sank
off the coast for the measurement of incentives

given through the French writings.
“we are rather satisfied,

investment bank Goldman Sachs
has struggled under steep

explosives trafficking,
as for many it represents

the persistent patterns
of the engines of integration.”

DEMOCRACY FORUM DIVIDED ON COUNTER-TERRORISM POLICY

secret electronic ballots,   that's the drag
on serving   as essential tools.

in the shared pain   of integration & housing,
a census of each child   must be getting the salaries

& calligraphy   already arrived by sea in
abstentions.   explanatory memorandum for

algae but even more so films   fiction with ourselves,
another failure.   fair share

barbed-wire fence along   the Kingdom has had very good
mineral resources, expedited trials,   & terror, he continued.

which forbid the use   of invitations
for doctors,   not only to freeze automobile victims

on the legs beneath expectations.   bicycle commuting measured
by gardens, or in proximity   to sharking the continent.

the material lives of its   sticking point for
we will use the proven track—   compassion for the devil

—fighting around the world,   our bodies, but also our
agreement to be rejected.   the assailants are

like many people—   rollerblading, trial biking,
army presents at the border,   this was not to resign

very happy about it, to work   toward the society free
of drug abuse.   a spire with the source

of criticism of Donald   to the benefit of the one
environmental cause   of cement, & aluminium,

her words were echoed   & the results of the session
were struck down   just prior to my truth.

STOP INCITING FEAR AND HATRED OF MIGRANTS, PLEAD REPRESENTATIVES

we were allocated a land plot, membership
fees, and accountability.
a grocery with unconfirmed mechanisms
to being good neighbours. these figures
in non-realist European progress.
it is a compensation.
my country is being harmed
right now. in the ranks of the political
catastrophic stupidity hurdles on.
this number could appear as if
papers are wrong.
everyone recently went bankrupt
in worrying, since,
after the growing schism
between its Cities in Solidarity
with Traffickers, there's talk
that what we try to say is
we died trying to escape
their parliament.
a billion per year in the population
slaughtered, like it was more necessary than ever,
people who belong to hand over their votes
to the intelligence-surveillance breakout feature,
in exchange for openness and growth

and high indications for food
and major infrastructure—
a part of the common world mess.
don't forget the food-processing industry,
in an effort to reach younger
or artificial flavours, have deactivated
weapons, and there is a love/hate
executive officer. violence only appears
to be preventing, and dealing groups have risen
in strength through exceptional compromises.
when they say no commenting
on the historic today,
to the current society we are islands
in the American "War on Terror."
but as memories of vulnerable people,
we praised the "cyclopsean" [sic]
surveillance, violent handshakes,
whenever there is a need.
the market of torture and death
must do more to fight
that deeply unflattering portrait,
reality. a new kind of iron it!
the market is growing,
the organ transplants worldwide
autumn session, a rise in divorce
proceedings, and I want that to be

the legacy disappeared today
following the abolition of religion,
but never my soul!
yes, we're proud of this,
but in compliance with the human
beings with the same bailout program,
officers should be sent
to a 3-year ceremony gathering
the tale of horror that they were:
depictions of the massacre, innocents
sacrificed for more investment.
Which Europe Now?
Europe to accept its elimination.
offered hope, secret for decades,
can explain many things.
natural resources. the festival.
those who think that following
the green light will engage
with online anthem.

PM DEMANDS INCREASED SECURITY MEASURES

carnations resistant to technology,
in green
and consisting of a single
delicate question
of police—

well,
in the labour market: more
police. that is the basis
of our lighthouse for future trade,
constructive and predictable.

the big picture is
a daily fact, a police check
with showers and bathrooms,
sugar, salt, fat, sweeteners,
technical assistance or
the stadium's bleachers.

and more like a ship
without "mutual enthusiasm"
loses its soul.

the union was dead.

they should never have
created an emotional painting,

there is no longer any valid
party to the conflict,
we have the
disproportionate share of
sheer madness.

the right-wing candidate is wrong
revenge, as in civil war
emissions.

this stability is violence,
every economy sitting here
destroys sea bed habitats and,
well,
in the central Mediterranean,
stormy debate,
the European project.
a clear and clean cut
from journalists.

a delivery deficit,
the great hypocrisy
of European philosophy
and literature, despite
the similar beginning.

humans and society
change, RESULTS
were the sign of fault lines
without us knowing in what.

but beyond the question of drowning
themselves in the viewer
with the bloody ordeal
perpetrators of the recent digital twin
should redouble efforts
to half that number of burial
school facilities.

Canada's role as a leader
concerns everyone,
and Copenhagen should be
ironized.

the people as of animals in
well. enditem.
become less human in that way?
we were left almost alone.

INTERNATIONAL HIGHLIGHTS: STORIES FROM AROUND THE GLOBE

I agree with something that is right.
The forces of secularism.
Antibiotics for cats.
Industry.
Mythology.
Latin.
An octopus with several parts.
I do not want the fairy to be traditionally resistant.
I do not want to eat food for your diet.
To die.
Give me the right path.
Mix my splendid apothecary pain.

*

There is a culture where there is silence.
Food, food, food and tea are allocated.
Copies of mirror banknotes.
Tin, stone, mouse.
Hypnotist phones.
According to the requirement of gardens.
Shangoosh is silent.
Evaluate the success of the mountains.
Which dive.
Prepared for a slow transition.

*

A good man is not obliged to work for local duties and responsibility.
Ask your husband about the problem.
He angered the army.
He sent the dead apostles.
An error is easy to facilitate.
The dead are dead, the dead are dead.
They support the most valuable neighbours for the construction of
the prison.
For the disappointment of unbelievers.
The radical geographical development of space.

Pay attention to the fascination of the good news.
Grand Slam Democratic Democracy Day.
Capitalism for the capitalization of Copenhagen.
Everything is revelling in the UK.
There are many opportunities to drink.
However, the euro is sad.
The communist spirit has changed the modernization of Germany.
Turkey's resistance is a useful tool.
The journalists were arrested by all means.
These violations began in November.
Moderators are still moving.
Soldiers try to suspect the sacred revolt.

*

You want racists to terrorize microchips?
Say something.
A strong voice is meaningful.
We will call the Parliament of Aragon.
Make sure the language is stronger to add a string.
To reduce the necessary control measures.
Disable unreadable pages.
Add 740 soprano to the theatre.
Without the canola industry.
Coffee is a password.
Find out while losing your milk.

*

There is no rigorous violence in a strong public.
However, some students are geographical traffickers.
Their works are interesting images.
There is a lot of damage to the productive dead.
Who have the presence of parliament.
The judge is against bones.
Burnt combustion brings conflict to save people from an explosion.
The sharper wind.
Real sound variants of the listener.
Special authorizations in the garden.
Animals are looking for you.
Therefore, you must die.
Happy Hollywood Suzhou.
Eline Eline Eline Eline.

FEATURE:
REFUGEE ACTION ON THE RISE

they arrive | the majority of refugees | stop the departure of Syrian refugees | police officers or still other refugees | for organisations working with refugees | to equitably redistribute the refugees | in the face of the crisis where several thousand refugees | in solidarity with the refugees | they arrive | the majority of refugees | with Greece where thousands of refugees | joins the network welcoming refugees | against the detention of refugees | Europe with thousands of refugees | they arrive | the majority of refugees | to bring assistance to the refugees | for assistance in handling refugees | the flux of over a million refugees | this time, some 46,000 refugees | to represent the bodies of refugees | receive over two years the Dublin Rule, which requires refugees | its policies and accept more refugees | with Syria where two million refugees | they arrive | the majority of refugees | aid and discuss taking up refugees | in the face of the crisis of refugees | Europe could not accept all refugees | massive influx of migrants and refugees | joins the network welcoming refugees | to receive and integrate the refugees | against the detention of refugees | better protection of female refugees | somewhere on the situation of refugees | where at least 2.2 million refugees | the specific needs of women refugees | Parliament to show support for refugees | promised to reduce the flow of refugees | receive over two years 30,000 refugees | promised to reduce the flow called for urgent and concerted action | already held many protest activities | in calling for action | to recruit youths who want action | be extended to include the activities | the entire world moves to action | also thrashed against the inaction | called attention to popular reaction | to try to attend the rally the chairman this year of the action | continued and met with similar action | a strong signal on environmental action | for urgent and concerted action | decisions | nothing excuses the inaction | customers, but coordinating our action | organisers of this symbolic action | coherence in the international activity | of empty rhetoric, concrete action | risks premature failure called for urgent and concerted action | nothing excuses the inaction | nothing excuses the inaction | of a long-planned terrorist action | the European External Action | look with vigilance at Frontex's action | risks premature failure | the reaction | urgent and incisive regulatory action | to recruit youths who want action | what it is," he said | he was reacting | to take concerted action | leading examples of an effective action | European Commissioner on Climate Action | the Group of Experts on Action | Commissioner for Action | they point out the only way to act | most important, however, are the actions | aims to transform the juridical act | to take more preventative action | European Parliament urges action | Paolo Gentiloni warned against inaction | on Human Rights and Democracy in Action | coherence in the international activity | participated in various activities | that the shared EU-Turkey action | be extended to include the activities | significant in the everyday activities | there must be swift action | of empty rhetoric, concrete action | will as the government's action | urgent and incisive regulatory action | risks premature failure | have a common responsibility to act | response to the reaction | to recruit youths who want action | in the Mediterranean: immediate action | coherence in the international activity | to establish a further course of action | online safe and legal avenues for refugees | into a transit country for refugees | they arrive | the majority of refugees | calling for urgent and effective action | in the interest of the refugees | the flux of over a million refugees | look with vigilance at Frontex's action | for the accommodation of refugees | more than one out of every two refugees | that receive the most refugees | to represent the bodies of refugees | the entire world moves to action | nothing excuses the inaction | to take more preventative action | to assist in the handling of refugees | this time, some 46,000 refugees | can Europe accept refugees | reminded the rapporteur to equitably redistribute the refugees | to receive and integrate the refugees | European Parliament urges action | to recruit youths who want action | there must be swift action | response to the reaction | risks premature failure for urgent and concerted action | Syrian, Iraqi and Eritrean refugees | participated in various activities | to recruit youths who want action | and their courage with the refugees | better protection of female refugees | to equitably redistribute the refugees | crossing in the sea | for urgent and concerted action | nearly 10,000 refugees | also thrashed against the inaction | this time, some 46,000 refugees | look with vigilance at Frontex's action | already held many protest activities | solidarity with international refugees | to take more preventative action | there must be swift action | there must be swift action | reminded the rapporteur | where several thousand refugees | and 11 in Finland | stop the departure of Syrian refugees | risks premature failure | to establish a further course of action | countries receive 86% of the refugees | this time, some 46,000 refugees | called for urgent and concerted action | called attention to popular reaction | that would stem the flow of refugees | receives the largest number of refugees | they arrive | the majority of refugees | conflict in the regions where refugees | promised to reduce the flow of refugees | to represent the bodies of refugees | for urgent and concerted action | risks premature failure | they arrive | the majority of refugees | crossing in the sea

LEADERS TO DEBATE FUTURE OF EUROPE

victorious or not next Sunday,
we share a passion
for political assassination,
though uniquely in order
to crisis.

for working
hours take their toll. the only way
to ensure we remain stupid
in the context
of the prognosis. solidarity.

later in the day, a suicide,
an external shock,
and that's transparency,
a rudder, south of the Italian island,
because simultaneous nature
and the "rendition" operations
held parts of the world.

all to change strategies,
the fatal shooting of 24
others, in a ceremony
to be held at numerous shocks,
"irregular payments" create
an enduring problem.

the story retells
the rights of children
in multi-speed Europe
optioned for a film.

lucky to live in peace,
the centre of the square,
I didn't know the word
novelty, let alone
a strong message, rather
since the double suicide
sticking point, the attacks,
which also have customers,
among other remedies,
the unsustainable.

the race will continue
on detrimental effects
from a wave of attacks and all
this seems like criticism
of massacre,
my characters' work.

we need more informed observers,
as well as silhouettes
on the ground
of peace; this is a lesson
that lives. that is
the basis of our origin.

I said, for these people
who I think
the problem is,
you French police
violence: disposal of the common
agreement, how many plants?
flowers and birds, provocations,
and among everywhere,
if not everyone,
a global crisis
that has no specialised shopkeeper.

to avoid disgusting slogans
the media move
forward. recognition by
this Syrian child
of which reception conditions
for manufacturing
of these the largest arms
producers, in high patronage of those
in the financial sector
with difficulties facing private life.

so by investing in a helping hand
to our "Brexit means Brexit" cartoons
mocking deep personal ethics,
others joke
and the Belgians shut their doors.
it's a win-win situation.
measuring how someone walks
into a huge cemetery.

DAVOS FORUM: ECONOMISTS ADVISE INCLUSIVE GROWTH

failure if politics do not
product. people's need to believe,
a bridge competition
in semi-automatics. however,
allow for the removal of life
in order to establish more
novelty,

in the eye-watering innocents
and sacrificed in companies, public
bodies and nationalisms,
reaching a recent low of 1.20
to be the sole authority
on the widely criticised
need to be continued.

experts on the fight against trade
will often highlight exhibition
in order for competitiveness between
the terrorist attacks.

in the midst of sheer chaos
at two factories
this has gone very well.
convincing, however,
remains littéraire.

every day, a degree
of cautious optimism resists
this system of authorising strikes,
criminal infraction and risks

of an isolationist anniversary
of the end of the Prince.

you cheap and green, clean
of new stained-glass windows.
all the international dangers have increased,
the robots were introduced
into migrants in Magyar lands.
recorded in histories of the flare
for criticism. the protection of life.
art under an ongoing freelance hand,
the ban on distribution, euro.
that's their pet
prize "to all the women,
all a series of homages
to the FBI investigation into one million inhabitants
of which prejudice has risen by 14%
hyping technology.

protestors walked down the would-be
catastrophe, for a qualifying exam.
it's as a vehicle
for better branches of Buddhism.

commentaries are legion,
even of Collective Against
Wings. no one knows how
the informal coffee shop meetings
protect minority languages,
together laid flowers
at the new normal around 6 to 7.

FEATURE:
CHINA IS THE FULL-VALUE CHAIN

China.
China only for
China. I mean,
China only for
China, and then
China, and then
China. So for us,
China. Before that,
China supply reform.
China in Europe, and
China. "People still see
China and is working for
China supports that, and
China," the CEO asserted.
China because people still see
China over 36 years. I lived in
China, it would be important for
China concerns everyone, and that
China, but for the world, based in
China's biggest trading partner, and
China, and then actually we realised
China." In particular, "Somewhere and
China, and therefore further growth in
China in 1980. I think, in that regard,
China and Switzerland). I do business with
China to address the World Economic Forum."
China, I certainly respect the President of
China in the global cinema industry. "Right now
China is an opportunity for Europe, not a threat
China, but for the world as well. The third thing,
China's economic perspective? I am strong believer in
China, it's more than 30%, in terms of turnover, and
China and India, he sees a more societal approach.
China wrongly as a place to produce, people still see
China, the Chinese Film Bureau, the Cultural Center of

China as a technology hub, we have patents registered in
China and it's important for the world. It's important for
China," as well as "access and inclusion in India." In both
China for the French public," he added, in recalling that
China, under the high patronage of the Ministry of Culture of
China and was one of the first European countries to recognize
China," declared Silvio Napoli to demonstrate the importance of
China is both a critical market and a hub for global operations.
China is the full value chain. We design elevators, not only for
China is the EU's second largest trading partner. The EU has been China's market economy status, to sign a free trade agreement with China's development over the last 36 years? We, definitely, accessed China and the first country to set up an industrial joint venture in China Unlimited established to celebrate 40 years of relations between China. It was only in 2009, however, when a friend invited him to visit China in 1980. It was also among the first European countries to recognize China, now we develop Chinese technology. There are very good engineers in China. We access it by trying to be the best that we can. We initially were in China both benefit from strong and stable bilateral ties. The European Union is China. And the most advanced products for elevators and escalators are made in China will soon have been at home there for almost a decade. The Consul General of China, and to apply for membership of the Asian Infrastructure Investment Bank, a China represents an external threat to Europe. This is untrue. In fact, the EU and China and Asia, based in Shanghai, was to convince people about the opportunity in China, it's something negative, like an earthquake." However, Davis recognizes that China in 2007. His research led him to write a new book, "Revitalising the Silk Road. China made its commitment to developing trade with the EU clear in March 2014 through China is the European country's largest trade partner in Asia. Since the inception of the China-EU comprehensive strategic partnership for mutual benefit and win-win cooperation." China, I think this is part of the Chinese integration. Part of my role when I was head of China has repeatedly shown in its partnerships with Europe. Through strong bilateral ties, China and France. "Every year we have nearly 6,000 French students going to study abroad in China at 6% is good. So I think the challenge – and I have full trust and full confidence in China will follow that route. It's also important, the environment is crucial, not only for China is 100 times bigger than our

small province. But I think I have the full confidence in China was one of the biggest obstacles on international climate negotiations, and look at now. China, even in my short period, has improved tremendously, so I can see this model is right for China as well. So we would not be able to have our worldwide position today if we had not been China will see a healthier situation in terms of pollution in the environment. Because Russia and China. Now I don't need to do this anymore, people believe in it. So then our goal is to continue supporting China's opening up to the global economy. Switzerland was one of the first countries to establish formal ties with China's future. Not only because I lived there and very much enjoyed living there, or because three children believe China trying to rapidly change it, and this is what part of the ten-year plan of President Xi, is, technology within China, because in Russia we can bring the green aluminium, our aluminium based on hydro-power energy, on the other hand China is also a very good hub to develop things for the whole world. Initially we imported technology from abroad into China and Europe should also work closer together in global governance issues, with climate change as a primary example. China who would go to invest and build a new tower in South America and ask us 'Why can't I get the same product I get in China has, I am convinced. One thing Mr. Xi reminded us yesterday was to say that the brave usually make a difference, and China for 11 years. And so I saw firsthand the progress, and I can relate to President Xi's comments. The life of people in China's inclusion in TISA talks, along with the goal of ensuring future "multilateralization" of the agreement. For its part, China grows maybe between 6.5 and 7%. I mean this is actually good. Of course, 10% was higher, but the global growth at 3% and China and its leadership, the five-year plan exactly addresses the right things. So the challenges are the Chinese reforms now bring China is the biggest elevator and escalator market in the world. It is more than 50%, so 1 in every 2 elevators sold worldwide is in China, Silvio Napoli was mixed with pride and hope." In 1980, it was a time when, I guess, no other company was prepared to believe in China in 1980. Starting with two factories, one in Suzhou and one in Shanghai, the Swiss company has grown during 37 years of business in China. His reasoning, he explained, was to show Chinese readers they have friends in France, and that rather than being an enemy of France China. So this has been a tremendous contribution. We do not disclose exact figures, but it is fair to say that Asia Pacific, which includes China for them is home, but also because I see what is happening. The biggest driver for elevator and escalator growth is urbanisation, and China is the biggest elevator and escalator market in the world, with more than 50% of elevators sold worldwide. This market has developed as China's market economy status, to establish a free trade agreement, and to apply for membership of the Asian Infrastructure Investment Bank, a China has also built up an enormous gene sequencing capacity, up to the point that many scientists in Europe and the U.S. send their samples to China-bashing in a way. In the 80s he was doing Japan-bashing. He seems to like to blame somebody else for economic problems in the US, but how China, he felt that such a gift was the strongest way to demonstrate his appreciation. The French painter did not always have a relationship with China. So we contribute also by developing technologies, by reinvesting in people, in assets, in technology, in green environmental technologies... China and its Tibetan province." To Chinese readers who already know his—

MORE HEADLINES LIKE THIS

Light licence shows enemies of air conditioning

133 days after returning to secret residence, a fast return

Irish trailer program suffers damage

DuPont clash over family development affects court decision

Bulgarian invaders show socialist PM ten passwords

Initiator began by occupying Chinese defence in Canada

Calendri's enemies threaten to coordinate fight

Establishment of religious award for religious medal

Thousands of bank accounts listed

National gov' only supports administration of logical admin

Cameron condemns wealth of fishermen

30 hours without noise

Penelope reduces value of important tax tax

Nazis deny minimum oil production in Latvia

Criticism of crisis accepted by critics

Alsace should go to work

The long wait at Auschwitz

100 days biological use increases heat of soul

Apple's last vice president Vladimir

Tektronix offers two protocols for second responsibilities

Financial fines still in Asia

Electromagnetic diplomats break skipper's lines to accommodate difference in military occupation

Austin starts Spielberg constitution, Moscow loses

Mapping algorithms independent of Finland

Flora adds wide range of methods

Stack of objections in Macedonia

Blair's hunger pension does not lie

Russian problem on real situations real

780 styles of images that transform unchanged unions of capitalism

Small light depends on future goals of green energy

Improving children in Tokyo improves Marrakesh

Your brother killed

Benefits of Syrian transit not lost

Amazon's ambassador covers environment, accuses tragedy of repenting

United States establishes DVD installation in explosion

Sun continues on May 24

MINISTERS CALL FOR INCREASED PROTECTION FOR WHISTLE-BLOWERS

important, how do we maintain flowers and birds,
tomorrow at risk to be a Twitter storm
away from fruitful science
and Chainsaw Massacre, two things pleasing
no one. Together, cinema politicians
have the abnormal campaign,
after the floral tie, of absent-mindedly battling
with private extensive surveillance,
up until now for "recreational" use. Enditem.
Now we see the gathering culture
we all share. And materials to do production
on the cultural front, on our novella-length story,
our architecture and works of art
constructed to rehouse
the world's seas and their non-road transport,
widened at the risk of walker. And many are those
artists exploring different social media sites,
and the risks of a "sanitary time
knowledge" as well as rock concerts.
This deep-sea country is able to face the ethical
discourses around remaining quiet and attentive,
to explain intimate technology, deafness,
species, and the people
more emotional than usual.

IMF WARNS AGAINST POLICY BLACK SWAN

her Russian counterpart,
did not arise yesterday.
but received however
unanimous fire
since the breaking
of our elevators
and our horizons,
from agriculture
to restrictions on mass
materials or of food—

we never turn our backs
on authorities, demanding
the creation of a win-win
cooperation strategy
in two boats
that six men were previously
and remain the backbone
of the study of issues
in Europe.

you have to dehumanise
the authorities,
"three wise men's gifts"
revealing multiple layers to
pay a "heavy price."

denounce the unkept,
for nothing will impede the
territorial disagreements
because we are neighbours.

is that the pharma industry
today, but how fast it grew.
you're a profit-driven
masterpiece. also planned
is a massive achievement,
following a failed military.

it is, of course, a moral case
called a "fool's bargain,"
responsible for the future
far from being certain.
because time is pressing.
two bomb explosions
rocked a really black swan.

to what extent are we
place.
rate.
book.
anymore.

Nazi remnants
have seen rapid growth
in the outside, insisted
again German police
in other words, it's tripled.
shocks no one.

what Europe is about?
will be revealed
on the radio and on
the solemn appeal against hate
Beethoven's 9th symphony

OP-ED: THIS CRISIS IS ABOUT CRISES OF VALUES

no one knows sanctuary in Europe
a taxi understood and inertia from
privacy breaches, terrorist attacks
by the artist for a share of the weighty well.
In my region, Octopus potential
solidarity about the future seeks to pump up
a legal arsenal because from day 1,
the celebrated strategy of importance
has been suffering new judges
on filmmakers, boys and girls
"I a statistical activity," said its provisions
quiet, pastoral for sure
clean up our mess?" is denied,
from sports to slaves
the illegal trade, tensions
in the hemicycle, education
Fin. Profound movements and
shared values which power plants,
the enjoyment of all
cultural radio show affairs at
the dismantlement resolution adopted
not happy with the public
television work he did during
the French artist schism
between its respect of intolerance and
buildings of the anéantie,
I have full trust regarding philosophical issues
seen as a refuge
with promises but projected onto the signs
with the child skeleton collection
on applause broke out

deep-sea fishing vessels needing authorities
to take off the "trending topic" on
imprisonment of the role in disruption
stands to be a human suffering process
We can January to return
in words, stripped of antipollution tests
position on ideological use bicycles,
but battles to light by any other Tuesday
"realistic" morphologies of doubts about
the prevention of a stormy debate
on the publication of the "of art"
this conundrum once presented on April policies."
there were secret parts of the growing
health extended to all the social whale hunting
Monday, the follow. The technology as competition.
transferred for law. Enditem. asylum.
deaths in the end of inheritance affirmed.
the deactivated, the painting
was following a tense a certain manner
"Of course be safe from
that would-be world,
Violent against existential want
leitmotifs,
the bigger and bigger factory in the
flux over a deafening silence
notably in Finland,
playing a key role in "the best friend which is home."
In a solemn admonished. The Uprising.
some citizens who live from the bigwigs
forced to ban retirement in a state of war.
first round of desire that
benefits to some very difficult victims
of the week-long session violation
of the combat people

consider how humans seem to have counterbalances
for tough questions. I breakthrough,"
simple purchases, targeted
new anti-torture festival of green
and animated the beyond biomedicine holidays
without secularism in Switzerland,
there is real disillusionment
"It is zones. Tin, globalisation, the somewhere
concerning the love of our own information
Bjork purchasing scheme people investments in the
international Ebola, lead to the
public. Fringe people. It's huge!" around the world
refugees who had weight and obesity
States as citizens these norms
taken in a test according to cinema luminaries
emergency quotas are left, which is
nevertheless the ability of the
read the book, the draft
countries signing do believe
there's an outside world, the Roma people
detention, and fierce criticism warned
against the collapse science decided
a police are penalization,"
reasonable, version are you crazy?
colourful insisting businessmen
who British Overseas
undermine the full French artists' interests."
another: is it Intellectual data
to parade down as a suitcase through capital
that was to enable drones
the death of things, so we hoping
that in gastronomy for their mutual
cinema fantastique abuse is supported
necessity to how asylum requests

the long term, "a violence must comprehensive trade
to define the "red are you crazy?
when tombs were made
a career a true migratory year.
whistle-blowers use experiments,
though orchestrated and held a long
coalition fighting days ago
in the negotiations to be discursive
the identity programs for milk
a consular building to the Roma
the cooperation of mass surveillance
the edge off a join.
it deaths from heart
to respect the bicycles
countries, notably full of dark, major effect,
often the night after depths of the self
especially for cotton, rapeseed
contested by awarding the viaducts
to some 2.7 million trans-fatty acid migrants
landing on significant policy alone is not Hugo
say in one breath Britain separating our lenders,
and we "blood minerals," pursue the truth
officially launched force.
The final structure was their own no
support from the better youth opportunities Commission,
drones the youngest have woes
declared to the child
the biggest problem in the world is geographers,
horror inflicted on deep-sea species in relationship."
all the social things we could do with
machine-propelled conscious laws
The progress people believe that
so with vegetables for discourse, people annexation
enormous proportion year that brought Kingdom.

Then the sudden questions on possible
difference between damages and solidarity."
Enditem cancelled." In May
which took place
in violation of probability,
having an easy time are happy because
calves, thick socks experts will join animals.
The report report", explained
need to improve alternatives.
Personally, I do writerly life and
in being attacked,
we had a kind of drinking water."

CORRECTIONS & RETRACTIONS

~~In their resolution, MEPs noted increased presence by Russia.~~

~~Russia, who has become the personae non grata in Europe since its annexation of Crimea in March 2014.~~

~~Russian annexation of Crimea in March 2014 viewed by the assembly as a "clear act of aggression" in violation with international law.~~

~~Russia's military intervention.~~

~~That the widely criticised Crimean referendum was illegal and insufficient grounds for Russia.~~

~~Russia, scheduled to host the 2018 World Cup, deemed by the EP to no longer to be a "strategic partner" for the EU.~~

~~With recent media reports claiming that Trump's campaign staff had frequent contacts with Russia.~~

~~Even while Mike Pence has told his European colleagues that the U.S. would "hold Russia accountable."~~

~~In light of ongoing conflict in Ukraine, as well as sanctions against Russia.~~

~~The Russian delegation to the US may be too fresh for European leaders to forget.~~

~~Suggesting the Americans were trying to meddle with the FIFA election.~~

~~A criminal investigation into the 2018 World Cup selection processes.~~

~~A mechanism in order to monitor financial assistance, political or technical, furnished by Russia.~~

~~However, international football might be seen as simply another opportunity to oppose Russia.~~

~~Russia and Qatar respectively.~~

~~Indicated that a better relationship with the Kremlin might be welcome.~~

~~Strasbourg adopted a resolution Wednesday calling for a more "realistic" strategy regarding Russia.~~

~~MEPs insisted on "EU relations with Russia."~~

~~And propose "investing more effort in dialogue with Russia."~~

~~In the long term, "a constructive and predictable relationship between the EU and Russia."~~

~~Russia and the West.~~

~~Russia and the United States.~~

~~Russia as a reliable partner and a responsible power.~~

~~"Europe needs Russia."~~

~~Russia and other parties on the situation in Syria, and the Paris Climate Agreement.~~

~~"Russia, China, Germany, France and Britain will say, you know what, this is a good deal, we're going to keep it."~~

~~Russia, judging that they will see a healthier situation in terms of pollution in the environment.~~

~~Russia, China, and their global partners have an opportunity to work on the problems, in order to see upward economic trends continue.~~

~~"Russia and China are natural neighbours, and we can do a lot together," he asserted.~~

~~Russia can bring the green aluminium.~~

~~Russia can be the natural supplier of commodities and materials to China, and then China can provide the further manufacturing of these materials for further stages.~~

~~Russia and China for political reasons.~~

~~Russia and China probably follow more conversations than the Stasi in East Germany was ever able to do with great resources and maybe a million informants.~~

~~Russian and Chinese companies.~~

~~Russia, and the former Soviet republics of Central Asia.~~

~~Russia played the role in brokering the deal between different producers in OPEC to achieve this agreement.~~

~~The Russian Federation, Sweden and the United States, as well as six organisations representing indigenous peoples.~~

~~Russia being until now in the ranks of those opposing such a resolution, could soften its position if it does not include reference to the destruction of vessels.~~

~~The situation in Syria since the entry into force of a fragile ceasefire negotiated by Russia.~~

~~The U.S. President has frequently praised Russia.~~

~~"We should not be involved in geopolitical point-scoring focused against Russia."~~

~~Russian President Vladimir Putin accused the US of trying to "extend its jurisdiction to other states."~~

~~As a reliable partner and a responsible power, but Russia.~~

~~The Arctic Council is made up of Canada, Denmark, Finland, Iceland, Norway, the United States, and the Russian Federation.~~

~~Russian military forces in the Arctic, which by 2015 "had established at least six new bases north of the Arctic Circles, including six deep-water ports and 13 airfields.~~

~~The Russian Duma Speaker, in a series of meetings organised to maintain open dialogue between the assembly and incident.~~

~~In a series of meetings organised to maintain open dialogue between the assembly and Russia.~~

~~"Russia implements the Minsk agreements in full," along with the fulfilment of other necessary conditions.~~

~~The Russian parliamentarian spoke at the meeting in a conciliatory tone, stressing the need for a political solution as the means to end violence.~~

~~Russia has been under tension.~~

~~Compounded by what seems to have been a complementary softening of U.S. positions toward Russia.~~

~~Russian authorities.~~

~~Russians known to intelligence services.~~

~~“Russia has to respect its international obligations for there to be peace, security and stability in Europe,” the President said.~~

~~“Russia has to accept that it is a party to the conflict,” he said, “and I hope it will shoulder its responsibility to solve it.”~~

~~Russia to take a more active role in ending unrest.~~

~~Russia ceased using what is also called "Double Summertime" in 2011.~~

~~The White Paper argues for the armament of the EU’s eastern neighbours, primarily against Russia.~~

~~“Russians should know that we defend our union with soft power as with hard power,” declared the representative.~~

~~Russia and a “less for less” policy towards “countries that try to throw democracy into reverse.”~~

~~Russian delegation’s credentials will be tabled early this week.~~

~~Russia had not passed a stress test.~~

~~Violations of the European Charter of Human Rights, such as those in April that suspended Russia.~~

~~Russia withdrew its representatives from the assembly for the rest of the year.~~

~~European Parliament calls on member states to avoid bilateral agreements with Russia.~~

~~Russian embargo, "could be useful for the farmers," even if "the budget set aside for fruit and milk distribution represents only 0."~~

~~The Russian Delegation does not have plans to leave the Council of Europe.~~

~~"Russia very important," he said during his introduction.~~

ENDITEM.

the end of this year. enditem. emissions
worldwide. enditem. violence
against women. enditem. but rather an iron will.
enditem. EU member states
as well. enditem. published last week. enditem.
quaestors on Wednesday. enditem.
the end of the war. enditem. and site visits. enditem.
and domestic violence. enditem. year's guest,
Vietnam. enditem. in the vicinity.
enditem. in Chinese universities.
enditem. by the European Union. enditem.
let it be understood. enditem. somewhere on Tuesday.
enditem. to end organ trafficking. enditem. development
in tourism. enditem. which to protect
them. enditem. our power to help
them. enditem. of the legal text. enditem.
in emissions testing. enditem. have been under tension.
enditem. Germany and Sweden. enditem.
and internet streaming. enditem. aid strategy.
enditem. hot water with Strasbourg. enditem.
by non-member states. enditem.
have historically showed. enditem. in all settings. enditem.
November plenary session. enditem.
considered separately. enditem. of asylum
seekers. enditem. Tibet and secularism. enditem.
for being scolded. enditem. on Human Rights. enditem.
and responsibilities. enditem. groups must respond.
enditem. minister to resign. enditem. Syrian
refugees. enditem. and urgent reforms.
enditem. drawn up for publication.
enditem. up with a new proposal. enditem.
and cultural programming. enditem. the negotiation

process. enditem. by Penguin
Press. enditem. and vice presidents.
enditem. if it is not postponed. enditem.
reconsider our position. enditem.
agriculture policy. enditem. it should come to pass.
enditem. the European Parliament.
enditem. attacks in Paris. enditem.
with a Chinese painter. enditem. posed
to be overwhelming. enditem. say otherwise.
enditem. three years of operation. enditem. be presented
in October. enditem. in Morocco in November. enditem.
these territories or not. enditem. ending
the negotiations. enditem. to kill
the naira. enditem. a height of 142 metres. enditem.
existing mechanisms. enditem. to new concrete
measures. enditem.
the risk of their lives. enditem. suspicion
of a link. enditem. on the national level. enditem.
cannot be above the law. enditem.
with the label. enditem. to be brought to justice.
enditem. Jean-Claude Juncker. enditem.
were imposed in January. enditem. 0.9%
of the food item. enditem. that fuels it.
enditem. will address the issue.
enditem. day on the Greek islands.
enditem. launched investigations. enditem.
a significant influence. enditem. the food industry. enditem.
international importance. enditem. asylum
and immigration. enditem. by illegality.
enditem. for the White House. enditem. the August
holidays. enditem. through local history. enditem. without hesitation.
enditem. Grand Chamber hearing. enditem. of the French
government. enditem. of state
and government. enditem. for the immediate future.

enditem. throughout France. enditem.
that of its founders. enditem. to enter
into force. enditem.
to enter into force.
enditem. to enter into force. enditem.
the migrants are fleeing.
enditem. whale fishing. enditem. party
to clean up FIFA. enditem. the annual European Fair.
enditem. and exploitation. enditem. 26,000 additional
events. enditem. on Wednesday evening. enditem.
250 million euros. enditem. trying to reach Europe.
enditem. the citizens of Europe.
enditem. partner for the EU. enditem.
and employment. enditem. of carbon emissions.
enditem. for its elimination. enditem. those
who are eligible. enditem. informed
once it is done. enditem.
but also to disconnect. enditem. in this direction.
enditem. sustainable development. enditem.
the medical decision. enditem. its consent
to the deal. enditem. in the last few days.
enditem. months after that date. enditem. research
and culture. enditem. affected
by the crisis. enditem. by organised crime.
enditem. participating countries.
enditem. expiration of a contract. enditem. rights,
she continued. enditem. people,
he continued. enditem. questions,
she concluded.
enditem. to share her concerns.
enditem. has filed a complaint.
enditem. the European Commission. enditem.
for his collection. enditem. the European coastlines.
enditem. will continue to close. enditem.

victims as civilians. enditem. refugees
being a child. enditem. Centennial
celebrations. enditem. table a new draft
budget. enditem. economy, and Brexit. enditem.
non-European behaviour. enditem. gain
in August. enditem. only 20 people attend.
enditem. in the two assaults. enditem. is expected
during April. enditem. and proposed amendments. enditem.
year's guest, Algeria. enditem. on Tuesday
afternoon. enditem. states in the affair. enditem.
and 51 abstentions. enditem. to 120 million
by 2020. enditem. its foundations in 1015. enditem.
enditem. enditem. enditem. enditem. enditem. enditem.
enditem. enditem. enditem. enditem. enditem. enditem.
enditem. enditem. enditem. enditem. enditem. enditem.
enditem. enditem. enditem. enditem. enditem. enditem.
enditem. enditem. enditem. enditem. enditem. enditem.
enditem. enditem. enditem. enditem. enditem. enditem.
enditem. enditem. enditem. enditem. enditem. enditem.
enditem. enditem. enditem. enditem. enditem. enditem.
enditem. enditem. enditem. enditem. enditem. enditem.
enditem. enditem. enditem. enditem. enditem. enditem.
enditem. enditem. enditem. enditem. enditem. enditem.
enditem. enditem. enditem. enditem. enditem. enditem.
enditem. enditem. enditem. enditem. enditem. enditem.
enditem. enditem. enditem. enditem. enditem. enditem.
enditem. enditem. enditem. enditem. enditem. enditem.
enditem. enditem. enditem. enditem. enditem. enditem.
enditem. enditem. enditem. enditem. enditem. enditem.
enditem. enditem. enditem. enditem. enditem. enditem.
enditem. enditem. enditem. enditem. enditem. enditem.
enditem. enditem. enditem. enditem. enditem. enditem.
enditem. enditem. enditem. enditem. enditem. enditem.

enditem. enditem. enditem. enditem. enditem. enditem.
enditem. enditem. enditem. enditem. enditem. enditem.
enditem. enditem. enditem. enditem. enditem. enditem.
enditem. enditem. enditem. enditem. enditem. enditem.
enditem. enditem. enditem. enditem. enditem. enditem.
enditem. enditem. enditem. enditem. enditem. enditem.
enditem. enditem. enditem. enditem. enditem. enditem.
enditem. enditem. enditem. enditem. enditem. enditem.
enditem. enditem. enditem. enditem. enditem. enditem.
enditem. enditem. enditem. enditem. enditem. enditem.
enditem. enditem. enditem. enditem. enditem. enditem.
enditem. enditem. enditem. enditem. enditem. enditem.
enditem. enditem. enditem. enditem. enditem. enditem.
enditem. enditem. enditem. enditem. enditem. enditem.
enditem. enditem. enditem. enditem. enditem. enditem.
enditem.

ABOUT THE AUTHOR

Jeremy Allan Hawkins is the French-American author of *Fantastic Premise* (Alien Buddha Press, 2023) and *A Clean Edge* (BOAAT, 2017), selected by Richard Siken as winner of the 2016 BOAAT Chapbook Prize. His poetry has been selected for the *Best New Poets* anthology series, and the extended program of the 2018 Venice Architecture Biennial.

PRAISE FOR THE AUTHOR AND WORK

Implausibly yet necessarily, *enditem.* shimmers with what could be called a 'poetics of logistics,' re-arranging and recasting the bureaucratic language of distribution and circulation into a language of transcultural revolution. Jeremy Allan Hawkins presents a portrait of 'the European project' that reveals the hypocrisy behind borders closed to bodies but open to markets, as well as tracks the role Global English plays in both distorting and codifying lived, local experience. However, Hawkins also shows us that ambivalence and malleability are written into the language, such that 'end item' becomes *enditem.*, less a finalized product for sale than the poetic imperative to keep connecting, configuring, and mobilizing.

—**Mia You,** author of *I, Too, Dislike It* (1913 Press, 2016)

Jeremy Allan Hawkins's collection *enditem.* employs collage to juxtapose pieces of current events – war, entertainment, commerce, geopolitical haggling and its human cost – against one another. Built with the language of news articles, Hawkins crafts a sharp portrait of our lived moment, vibrating with the 'uncertainties that persist,' and 'political catastrophic stupidity' of global proportions. This project emphasizes the schism between our felt and lived realities, amid the ongoing violence of wars, displaced communities, destruction. Readers will find themselves entranced with the language we are fed, only to have it reveal itself as poem, riddle, and ouroboros.

—**Avni Vyas,** author of *Little God* (Burrow Press, 2021)

Using techniques regularly applied in found poetry and avant-garde writing and superimposing them on his own past texts Jeremy Allan Hawkins executes a rare act of poetic emancipation towards the hegemonic discourses of our time and their echoes in our own voices and writing. *enditem.* is a disruptive piece of textual technology, elegant in its realization, intensely stimulating in its conceptual provocations and infinitely entertaining in its innovation.

—**Robert G. Elekes**, author of *O dronă care să mă vrea în sfârșit doar pe mine (a drone that will finally love me)*, Max Blecher Publishing House, 2018)

www.ingramcontent.com/pod-product-compliance
Lightning Source LLC
Chambersburg PA
CBHW011148290426
44109CB00023B/2532
9780645231878